Discover Writing Discover Korea 10

[여는 말]

한국에는 수준 높은 좋은 영어 교재들이 많이 있습니다. 그러나 이들 중 대부분의 책들은 한국 학생들의 삶과 문화에 진정으로 연결되어 있지 않고, 외국 문화와 맥락으로 가득 차 있습니다. 학생들이 교재의 내용에 공감하지 못해 영어에 대한 관심을 잃는 것을 보며 이러한 의문들이 들기 시작했습니다. "만약 한국 문화를 중심으로 한 교제가 있다면 어떨까?", "만약 교재가 학생들의 일상 생활과 더 밀접하게 연결되어 있다면 어떨까?".

이렇게 시작된 "만약"은 "나도 어쩌면 작은 변화를 가져올 수 있다."는 생각의 씨앗이 되었습니다. 모든 것을 바꿀 방법은 없을지도 모르지만, 제가 시작점이 되어 한국 학생들을 위한, 한국 문화를 반영한 영어 학습 자료, 그리고 학생들에게 친숙하고 위로가 되는 학습자료를 제공하고 싶었습니다.

Discover Writing Discover Korea 시리즈는 **총 10 권**으로 구성되어 있습니다. 이 시리즈는 제목에서도 선명하게 보이듯이 영어 글쓰기를 위한 책입니다. 이 10 권의 책시리즈들은 **각 장르별 영어 글쓰기 스킬을 제공**하면서 동시에 **다른 책에서 다루지 않는 문법의 일면들을 제공**하고 있습니다. 이 책을 통해 또한 **학생들은 자기평가가 가능**합니다. 보통의 교실환경에서 학생들은 주로 평가를 받는 입장입니다. 학생들은 점수에만 매인 채 평가의 의미와 결과의 이유는 잘 알지 못합니다. 이 책에서는 학습자가 평가의 주체가 되어 봄으로서 새로운 시각으로 본인의 글을 볼 수 있는 기회를 제공합니다. 학습자들은 **친숙한 한국문화**를 밑바탕으로 낯선 컨텐츠에 방해받지 않고 쓰기학습이라는 **본연의 목적에 충실**할 수 있도록 설계되었습니다.

저는 **진정한 영어 글쓰기를 위한 쓰기교육**을 학생들이 이 책과 함께 이루어 나가길 소망합니다. 학생들이 이 책에 빠져들며 영어 글쓰기 실력을 향상시키고 진정한 학습의 기쁨을 맛볼 수 있기를 진심으로 바랍니다.

이 책이 만들어지기까지 항상 용기를 주었던 나의 가족들, 학교 동기 선생님들, 교수님들, 친구들 그리고 나의 학생들과 학부형님 모두에게 감사 인사를 드리고 싶습니다.

나의 고민을 함께해주며 같이 울고 웃어준 나의 남편, 전화한통도 조심스러웠던 양가 부모님과 표지 제작에 많은 도움을 준 내 동생, 항상 용기를 주시고 나의 가치를 인정해 주셨던 성희선생님과 지선선생님, 그리고 소중한 오랜 인연 해정님, 멋진 코믹을 사용할 수 있게 기회를 열어 주신 PIXTON, 지금의 책이 있을 수 있게 열정적인 조언을 주셨던 정은영 교수님과 박혜옥 교수님, 그리고 누구보다 나의 발전에 불을 지피고 영감을 주며 지켜봐 주신 Chris 교수님께 special thanks 를 드리고 싶습니다.

[Prologue]

In Korea, there are many high-quality English textbooks available. However, most of these books are not genuinely connected to the lives and culture of Korean students; they are filled with foreign contexts and cultures. It saddened me to see students unable to relate to the content of these textbooks, causing them to lose interest in learning English. This raised questions in my mind: "What if there were materials centered around Korean culture?" "What if textbooks were closely linked to students' daily lives?"

These "what ifs" planted the seed of the thought, "Perhaps I can make a small change." While I may not be able to change everything, I wanted to be the starting point for providing English learning materials that reflect Korean culture and are familiar and comforting to students.

The "Discover Writing Discover Korea" series is comprised of a total of 10 volumes. As clearly indicated by its title, this series is a book for English writing. These ten volumes offer English **writing skills specific to various genres while also providing aspects of grammar not covered in other books.** Through this series, **students can also conduct self-evaluation**. In typical classroom environments, students are usually on the receiving end of evaluations. They are often bound to scores, not fully understanding the meaning of the evaluations or the reasons behind their results. This book gives learners the opportunity to become the evaluators themselves, allowing them to see their writing from a new perspective. The series is designed so that learners can remain true to the fundamental goal of writing education without being hindered by unfamiliar content, **based on the familiar backdrop of Korean culture.**

I hope that students embark on a journey of true English writing education with these books. I sincerely wish for them to immerse themselves in these books, improve their English writing skills, and experience the true joy of learning.

I would like to express my gratitude to my family, schoolmates, teachers, friends, and all my students and fellow educators who have always supported me in the creation of this book.

To my husband, who shared my concerns and laughed and cried with me, to my cautious parents who were always just a phone call away, to my younger sister who provided invaluable assistance in designing the cover, to Seonghee and Jisun, who always encouraged me and recognized my worth; to my precious long-time friend, Hae-jung; to PIXTON for opening the opportunity to use amazing comics, to Professor Eun-young Jeong and Professor Hye-ok Park, who provided passionate advice and most importantly, to Professor Chris Douloff, who has been a source of inspiration, guidance, and unwavering support in my personal growth—special thanks to you all.

ORGANIZATION OF THE BOOK

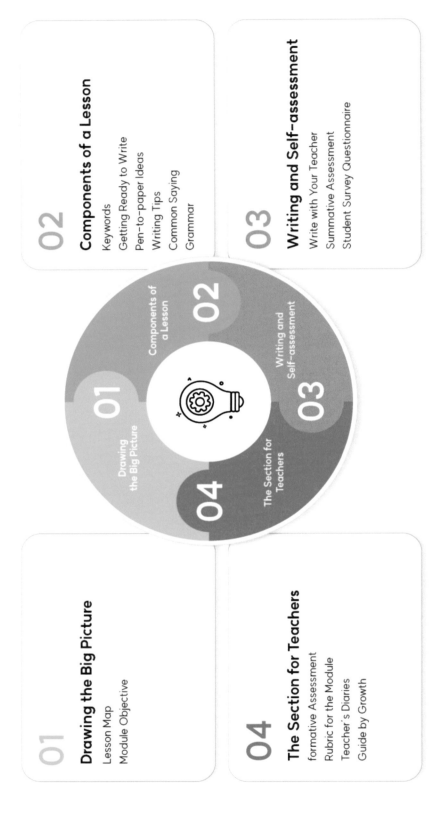

01 Drawing the Big Picture
Lesson Map
Module Objective

02 Components of a Lesson
Keywords
Getting Ready to Write
Pen-to-paper Ideas
Writing Tips
Common Saying
Grammar

03 Writing and Self-assessment
Write with Your Teacher
Summative Assessment
Student Survey Questionnaire

04 The Section for Teachers
formative Assessment
Rubric for the Module
Teacher's Diaries
Guide by Growth

INTRODUCTION OF TLC, GENRE WRITING, AND PROCESS WRITING

The teaching-learning cycle, genre writing, and process writing are three effective methods that interrelate and complement each other in fostering students' writing skills.

1. Teaching-Learning Cycle (TLC)

The Teaching-Learning Cycle is a systematic approach to teaching that involves four stages: **building the field** (contextualizing and building background knowledge), **modeling** (showcasing examples), **joint construction** (collaborative writing), and **independent construction** (students write on their own).

Relation to Other Methods: TLC acts as a framework where genre writing and process writing can be incorporated. For example, while modeling, you can introduce different genres and engage students in the process of writing stages.

Application: Start by engaging students with images or discussions to build context (**Building the Field**). Then, provide a well-structured example text (**Modelling**), followed by collaborative writing (**Joint Construction**). Finally, allow students to write independently.

2. Genre Writing

Genre writing focuses on teaching students about different text types or genres such as narratives, reports, or persuasive texts, and **the language features and structures commonly used** in each.

Relation to Other Methods: Within the TLC, different genres can be modeled and practiced. Process writing can be applied within a specific genre to go through the drafting, revising, and editing stages.

Application: Choose a **genre** and **model a text**, discussing its **specific language features** and **structures**. Then, **guide** students to write their own texts following the conventions of the chosen genre.

3. Process Writing

Process writing emphasizes the steps or processes in writing such as planning, drafting, revising, editing, and publishing.

Relation to Other Methods: It can be embedded within the TLC during the independent construction phase and can be utilized across different genres.

Application: Guide students through each stage, from brainstorming ideas (**Planning**), writing a first draft (**Drafting**), getting and giving feedback (**Revising**), correcting errors (**Editing**), to finally publishing their work.

The integration of these three methods offers a **comprehensive, structured, and student-centered approach to teaching writing**, which supports students in becoming autonomous, reflective, and proficient writers.

TABLE OF CONTENTS

Lesson Map

MODULE 10: A SPEECH SCRIPT WRITING						
	GET READY TO WRITE			WRITE		REVISE & EDIT
KEYWORDS	MODEL TEXTS	PEN-TO-PAPER IDEAS & WRITING TIPS	GRAMMAR	WRITE WITH YOUR TEACHER	WRITE BY YOURSELF	EDITING
Unforgettable, relationship, memorable, sightseeing, support, throughout, meaningful, fulfill, connect, intimidating	IT WAS A TRULY EYE-OPENING EXPERIENCE FOR ME.	• understand the features of a speech script. • organize a script considering the frame of a speech script • apply proper examples experience and opinions in a script • Common Saying: *an eye-opening experience*	• M dash • present perfect tense	• completing the unfinished part of an instruction	• challenge: write a speech script under the given prompts	• check an m dash

Example Lesson Plans: Module 1 [8 classes, 6 hours]

Module objectives ⭐ **2**	*By the end of* **Module 1**, *a student will be better able to*
	O1. compose a self-introduction using simple, short sentences, and a first-person perspective considering the readership and purpose of the text. **O2.** understand language in chunks and fixed expressions **O3.** share personal information safely and appropriately, and use the appropriate tone. **O4.** apply simple vocabulary and present tense **O5.** understand the rules of the S-V agreement and apply them in writing.
Legend	TLC = Teaching learning cycle
Class 1	TLC stage: *Modelling*
Major Stages	**1.** Explain module objectives to S
	2. "Task A" (1–5): Have S read questions and discuss.
	3. "KEYWORDS": Have S check the target words and elicit their meaning. Help S pronounce words correctly. If needed, use **MORE EXERCISE FOR KEYWORDS**
	4. "Model Text": Have S read the given cartoon and understand the context. Give S a "Model Text" and encourage S to notice the target words in the text. Have S understand the content of the text using concept-checking questions (CCQ).
HW	**"HOMEWORK DAY 1"**
Class 2	TLC stage: *Modelling*
Major Stages	1. 1. **"HOMEWORK DAY 1"**: to check + **"KEYWORDS"**: to review + **"Model Text"**: to review
	"WRITING STRATEGIES—"Writing Process"**: Have S read and discuss.
	1. **"DEEP DIVE"**: Have S analyze **"Model Text"**. Have S consider the structure. S applies to **"DEEP DIVE A & B"**. If a learner doesn't have a partner, the teacher fills that role as a guide. Don't forget that the teacher's role is not only to teach but also to observe, and guide
HW	**"HOMEWORK DAY 2"**
Class 3	TLC stage: *Modelling*

Major Stages	1. "HOMEWORK DAY 2": to check + "KEYWORDS": to review + "Model Text": to review
	2. KEY ELEMENT & TIPS—"Self-introduction Etiquette"(Tip 1–6): to check S understands tips for writing self-introduction. Have S complete "EXERCISE 1, 2", "HANDS-ON ACTIVITIES A, B", and "DEEP DIVE A, B".
	3. "SUMMARY": to review a letter-writing process
HW	"HOMEWORK DAY 3"
Class 4	TLC stage: *Modelling*
Major Stages	1. "HOMEWORK DAY 3": to check + "KEYWORDS": to review + "Model Text": to review + "Self-introduction Etiquette"(Tip1-6): to review
	2. KEY ELEMENT & TIPS —Fixed Expression: Have S read examples and elicit the expression's meaning. Have S solve "EXERCISE 3–5".
	3. "DEEP DIVE": Have S read "Model Text" and analyze the fixed expression in the text.
HW	"HOMEWORK DAY 3"
Class 5	TLC stage: *Modelling*
Major Stages	1. "GRAMMAR 1": Have S think about when to use the present tense. Have S read "GRAMMAR 1" and provide some time to notice the function of the present tense. Have S solve "EXERCISE 6". Conduct CCQ.
	2. "DEEP DIVE A-D": Have S read "Model Text" and analyze.
	3. "HANDS-ON ACTIVITIES A, B: Have S solve.
HW	"HOMEWORK DAY 5"
Class 6	TLC stage: *Modelling*
Major Stages	1. "HOMEWORK DAY 5": to check + "KEYWORDS": to review + "Model Text": to review + Self-introduction Etiquette (Tip1-6) to review + "Fixed Expression": to review + "GRAMMAR 1": to review
	2. "GRAMMAR 2-1": Have S think about the rule of present Be-verb. Have S read "GRAMMAR 2-1". Have S solve "EXERCISE 7". Conduct CCQ.
	2. "GRAMMAR 2-2": Have S think about the rule of present Action-verb. Have S read "GRAMMAR 2-2". Have S solve "EXERCISE 8". Conduct CCQ.

	3. "**HANDS-ON ACTIVITIES**": S makes sentences in "HANDS-ON ACTIVITIES A, B".
HW	"**HOMEWORK DAY 6**"
Class 7	TLC stage: *joint construction1–2*
Major Stages	1. "**HOMEWORK DAY 6**": to check + "**KEYWORDS**": to review + "**Model Text**": to review + **Self-introduction Etiquette (Tip1-6)** to review + "**Fixed Expression**": to review + "**GRAMMAR 1**": to review "**GRAMMAR 1**": to review +"**GRAMMAR 2-1, 2-2**": to review
	2. "**WRITE WITH YOUR TEACHER 1**": Have S understand the purpose of the task. Guide S to complete the unfinished text. Demonstrate S how to revise and edit using the checklist.
	3. "**WRITE WITH YOUR TEACHER 2**": Have S understand the task's purpose and demonstrate the process writing procedure. Complete the task with S.
HW	"**HOMEWORK DAY 7**"
Class 8	TLC stage: *Independent construction*
Major Stages	1. "**HOMEWORK DAY 7**": to check + "**KEYWORDS**": to review + "**Model Text**": to review + **Self-introduction Etiquette (Tip1-6)** to review + "**Fixed Expression**": to review + "**GRAMMAR 1**": to review "**GRAMMAR 1**": to review +"**GRAMMAR 2-1, 2-2**": to review + "**WRITE WITH YOUR TEACHER 2**": to review the procedure of process writing
	2. "**INDEPENDENT WRITING**": Have S understand the purpose of the task. Have S look through and complete the task.

MODULE OBJECTIVES

In this module, you will learn how to

- organize the text in a speech text structure

- analyze the elements of each part

- explain a writer's thoughts and claims with evidence

- analyze methods for delivering speeches effectively

- understand the procedures of pre-writing, drafting, revising, and editing.

A.   Answer the questions. Discuss with your partner.

1. Have you tried to make people agree with your opinions and thoughts?
2. What strategies did you use for it?
3. What did you feel when people finally accepted your thoughts and opinions?

KEYWORDS

Match the words with pictures. Check the meanings and pronunciation with your teacher.

Last weekend, my family and I went _____ in the city. We visited the museum, the park, and the old castle.

- • unforgettable

The letter from best friend was very _____ because it showed how much she cared about our friendship.

- • relationship

My birthday party was _____ because all my friends came, and we had so much fun playing games and eating cake.

- • memorable

Helping my friend with her project made me feel happy because I was able to _____ my promise to support her.

- • sightseeing

The school trip to the zoo was _____ because we saw so many amazing animals and learned a lot about them.

- • support

I have a good _____ with my brother. We play together and help each other with homework.

- • throughout

- • meaningful

- • connect

- • fulfill

- • intimidating

MORE EXERCISE FOR KEYWORDS

Exercise 1. Check the meaning of each word above again. Put them with the word that takes the same role in each box together. Work with your partner. Follow an example.

e.g., apple, bus, cat...	e.g., pretty, soft, big...	e.g., eat, have, run...

Exercise 2. Check the pronunciation and stress of each word. Work with your partner. Follow an example.

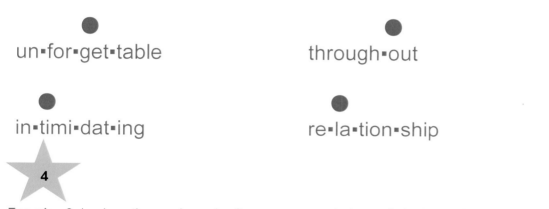

un▪for▪get▪table

through▪out

in▪timi▪dat▪ing

re▪la▪tion▪ship

★ **4**

Exercise 3. Look up the words again. Can you guess what story is in the text? Discuss with your partner.

MORE EXERCISE FOR KEYWORDS

Exercise 4. Fill in the gap with the words below.

Unforgettable, relationship, memorable, sightseeing, support, throughout, meaningful, fulfill, connect, intimidating

1. When we went to Paris, we did a lot of _____. We visited the Eiffel Tower, the Louvre Museum, and many other famous places.

2. My birthday party was very _____ because all my friends came, and we had a great time playing games.

3. I felt happy _____ the entire day of the school trip because I was with my friends and we learned so many new things.

4. My best friend and I have a great _____. We always help each other with homework and have fun together.

5. I felt a sense of _____ when I finished reading my first big book. It was a great achievement for me.

6. My parents always _____ me when I have a difficult task at school. They encourage me and help me succeed.

7. Helping my little brother with his homework was a _____ experience. It made me feel proud and happy.

8. Speaking in front of many people can be very _____, but I know I can do it with some practice and confidence.

9. In our new class project, we will _____ with students from other countries to learn about their cultures and traditions.

10. Last summer, I had an _____ trip to the mountains with my family. We saw beautiful waterfalls and hiked through amazing forests.

11. My family and friends always _____ me when I have a problem or need help.

12. I want to _____ my dream of becoming a scientist by studying hard and doing well in school.

13. Speaking in front of the whole class can be _____, but practice can help you feel more confident.

14. The trip to the amusement park was _____ because I had so much fun with my friends.

15. _____ the year, we have many holidays and celebrations to enjoy.

MODULE 10   WHAT SHALL I DO TO WRITE A SPEECH?

Sally is sad because her summer vacation is going to be over soon. Now, she meets her friend A-young and they are talking about how to make the rest of her time in Korea meaningful.

Comic made at Pixton.com

Comic made at Pixton.com

Model Text

Title
: The title captures the essence of the speech and the main theme. A title reflects the main topic or lesson of your speech.

The Sparkling Journey in Korea: The Power of Relationships

Body
The body is where the main points and supporting details of the speech are presented. It is usually divided into several paragraphs, each focusing on a specific point.

Part 1

: This part introduces the initial experience and sets up the role of the uncle in the narrative. Describe your initial feelings and the support you received from someone important.

Good afternoon, everyone,

Today, I am here to share with you a story of an unforgettable summer vacation that taught me the true value of relationships. My name is Sally. This summer, I had the amazing opportunity to visit Korea because my uncle works there as an English teacher.

When I arrived in Korea, I was excited but also a bit nervous. I wondered how I would navigate this new place and culture. Thankfully, my uncle was there to guide me every step of the way. When my grandmother visited me, I worried about which places to take her to. My classmate at the Korean language school helped me plan the perfect itinerary, suggesting places like Gyeongbokgung Palace, Gwangjang Market, and Namsan Tower. His advice made our time together even more memorable. It was a truly eye-opening experience for me.

In addition to sightseeing, I started learning Korean at a language school. My teacher was incredibly kind, and my classmates were always ready to help me. Their support made learning fun and less intimidating. I also made a new friend through language exchange. We helped each other learn, shared our cultures, and became close friends. According to a study by the American Psychological Association, social support can reduce stress by up to 55%, which I certainly experienced. Throughout my journey in Korea, I realized that the people around me made all the difference.

My uncle, grandmother, classmates, and friends supported me every step of the way. They turned my worries into confidence and my fears into excitement.

Conclusion
: The conclusion reinforces the main message and leaves the audience with a powerful takeaway.

This experience taught me that relationships are the most important part of any journey. Without these wonderful people, my time in Korea would not have sparkled as brightly. They showed me that life is richer and more meaningful when shared with others.

Introduction

: The introduction sets the stage, introduces the speaker, and provides context for the story. Greet your audience, introduce yourself, and give a brief overview of what your speech will be about.

Part 2

: This part elaborates on the support from the teacher, classmates, and a new friend, emphasizing the importance of relationships using a scientific fact. Describe the ongoing support you received from multiple people and how it positively impacted your experience.

Part 3

: This paragraph reflects on the overall importance of relationships in the speaker's experience. Summarize the key lesson learned from the experiences and the role of relationships.

Restate the main lesson, summarize your key points, and end with an inspirational message.

In conclusion, I learned that good relationships are the key to a fulfilling life. Whether it's family, friends, or teachers, the people we connect with shape our experiences and help us grow. So, cherish your relationships, support each other, and remember that together—we can make every moment sparkle.

Thank you for listening, and I hope you all find the same joy and support in your relationships as I have in mine.

감사합니다!

Closing
: The closing thanks the audience and ends the speech on a positive note. Thank your audience for their attention and give a final, warm farewell. If relevant, include a phrase in another language to connect with the audience.

Comic made at Pixton.com

Comic made at Pixton.com

What is a SEVOC in a speech script?

: **SEVOC** is essential in writing a speech script because it helps create an engaging, clear, and effective message that resonates with the audience. Here's what each feature is and why they are important.

▪ Start Strong

Importance:

- **Captures Attention:** An interesting fact, question, quote, or story immediately grabs the audience's attention, making them more likely to listen attentively.
- **Sets the Tone:** A strong start sets the tone for the entire speech and prepares the audience for what's to come.
- **Engages Emotionally:** Starting with a relatable story or intriguing fact can engage the audience emotionally, making the speech more impactful.

▪ Engage with Stories and Examples

Importance:

- **Makes Points Vivid:** Personal anecdotes and relatable examples make abstract points more concrete and easier to understand.
- **Enhances Memorability:** Stories are more memorable than dry facts. They help the audience remember the key points of the speech.
- **Builds Connection:** Sharing personal experiences creates a connection between the speaker and the audience, fostering empathy and engagement.

- ## Use Visual Aids Wisely

Importance:

- **Clarifies Information:** Visual aids can help explain complex ideas and data more clearly than words alone.
- **Enhances Retention:** People remember visual information better, so using charts, slides, or props can make the speech more memorable.
- **Keeps Interest:** Visual aids can keep the audience's attention and make the speech more dynamic.

- ## Organize Clearly

Importance:

- **Ensures Flow:** A logical order helps the speech flow smoothly, making it easier for the audience to follow and understand the message.
- **Highlights Key Points:** Clear organization ensures that the main points are highlighted and not lost in a jumble of information.
- **Aids Comprehension:** Transitions between sections help the audience see the connections between different points, enhancing comprehension.

- ## Be Concise

Importance:

- **Maintains Focus:** Being concise ensures that the speech stays focused on the main message without unnecessary digressions.
- **Respects Audience's Time:** A concise speech respects the audience's time and keeps their attention by avoiding unnecessary details.
- **Enhances Impact:** Clear and to-the-point sentences make the speech more powerful and impactful, leaving a stronger impression on the audience.

Comic made at Pixton.com

• Start Strong:

Use an interesting fact, a question, a quote, or a short story to capture the audience's attention at the beginning.

Interesting Fact:
e.g., Did you know that the average person spends about two hours a day on social media?

Question:
e.g., Have you ever wondered what it would be like to live without electricity for a day?

Quote:
e.g., Albert Einstein once said, 'The only source of knowledge is experience.'

Short Story:
e.g., When I was ten, I accidentally planted a seed in my backyard, and to my surprise, it grew into a beautiful tree that still stands today.

• Engage with Stories and Examples:

Use personal anecdotes, stories, and relatable examples to make your points more vivid and memorable.

e.g., I remember a time when I struggled with math. It was only after my teacher shared a fun math game with me that I began to enjoy and understand it.

▪ Use Visual Aids Wisely:

If using slides, charts, or props, ensure they are clear, relevant, and enhance the speech rather than distract from it.

e.g., Here's a simple chart that shows how recycling can reduce waste by 50%. As you can see, the impact is significant.

▪ Organize Clearly:

Use a logical order for your points (chronological, problem-solution, cause-effect, etc.). Make transitions between sections clear to help the audience follow your ideas.

Chronological:
e.g., First, we will look at the history of recycling. Then, we will examine its current practices. Finally, we will explore future innovations.

Problem-Solution:
e.g., Pollution is a growing problem. One solution is increasing our recycling efforts.

Cause-Effect:
e.g., Using plastic bags leads to pollution. This pollution harms marine life.

▪ Be Concise:

Avoid unnecessary words or tangents. Keep your sentences and paragraphs short and to the point.

e.g., Instead of saying, 'At this point in time, we need to consider the possibility of starting to recycle more,' say, 'We need to start recycling more now.'

!

DEEP DIVE

A. Look at the model text. Then answer the questions.

1. What genre does the text belong to?

2. What is the purpose of the text?

3. How many parts are in the text? Can you explain the function of each part?

B. Look at the model text. Then answer the questions.

1. Who was the reader of the text?

2. Who was the writer?

3. How close is the reader and the writer? How do you know it?

4. Find one example that shows the relationship between the reader and the writer from the model text.

C. Fill in the blanks with the body parts. Read the text below and circle the writer and reader. Then underline the purpose of this text.

The Importance of Recycling: Protecting Our Environment and Saving Resources } _____

Good afternoon, everyone. Today, I want to talk to you about something very important: recycling. My name is Hyun-young, and I am here to discuss how recycling can help protect our environment. } _____

Firstly, let me tell you about why recycling is essential. For example, did you know that recycling one ton of paper can save 17 trees? This simple action can make a big difference.

Another important point is that recycling reduces pollution. According to scientists, recycling plastic saves up to 88% of the energy required to produce plastic from raw materials. } _____

Lastly, let's consider how recycling can save money. Many communities earn money by selling recycled materials, which can be used to fund local projects.

In conclusion, recycling is crucial for protecting our environment, reducing pollution, and saving money. Let's remember that small actions like recycling can have a big impact. } _____

Thank you for listening. I appreciate your time and attention. Let's all work together to make recycling a part of our daily lives. Have a great day } _____

Comic made at Pixton.com

TIP 1   **TITLE**

The title captures the essence of the speech and gives the audience an idea of the main topic.

Common Expressions:
e.g., The Importance of [Topic]
e.g., How [Topic] Can Change Our Lives
e.g., The Power of [Topic]

8 Good example ✓	Bad example X
The Importance of Recycling: Protecting Our Environment and Saving Resources	Recycling Stuff
This title is clear and informative, indicating the main focus of the speech and its significance.	This title is vague and does not clearly indicate what the speech will be about.

EXERCISE 1. Read the short speech scripts below. Then, create a suitable title for each speech that captures the main idea. Follow the example.

e.g., Good morning, everyone. Today, I want to talk to you about the importance of recycling. Recycling helps save resources, reduce pollution, and protect our environment. By recycling paper, we can save trees. Recycling plastic saves energy. Let's all do our part to make the world a cleaner place.

Your Title: The Power of Reading: Benefits of Books

Speech script 1. Good afternoon, everyone. Today, I want to share why reading books is so beneficial. Reading improves our knowledge, helps us relax, and expands our imagination. Books are like friends that teach us new things and take us to exciting places. Let's make reading a part of our daily routine.

Your Title:_____

Speech script 2. Good afternoon, everyone. Today, I want to discuss the benefits of eating healthy. Eating fruits and vegetables gives us energy and keeps our bodies strong. A balanced diet helps us stay focused and feel good. Let's choose healthy foods to improve our lives.

Your Title: _____

The introduction grabs the audience's attention, introduce yourself, and present the main topic.

Common Expressions:
e.g., Good [morning/afternoon/evening], everyone.
e.g., Today, I want to talk to you about something very important: [Topic].
e.g., My name is [Your Name], and I am here to discuss [Topic].

Five different ways of introduction	Example
1. Starting with a Question	Good morning, everyone. **Have you ever wondered why recycling is so important?** My name is Sarah, and today, I want to talk to you about how recycling can help protect our planet.
2. Using an Interesting Fact	Good afternoon, everyone. **Did you know that recycling one ton of paper can save 17 trees?** My name is Ha-young, and today, I want to talk to you about the importance of recycling.
3. Sharing a Personal Anecdote	Good afternoon, everyone. **When I was younger, I didn't enjoy reading. But one day, I found a book that changed my life.** My name is Joo-ri, and today, I want to share with you the power of reading.
4. Quoting a Famous Person	Good afternoon, everyone. **Albert Einstein once said, 'The only source of knowledge is experience.'** My name is Hannah, and today, I want to talk about the importance of hands-on learning.
5. Stating the Purpose Directly	Good morning, everyone. **Today, I want to talk to you about something very important: the benefits of recycling.** My name is Eun-ha, and I am here to discuss how recycling can help protect our environment.

EXERCISE 2. Read the introduction above. Match an appropriate introduction way with each introduction. Follow the example.

Starting with a Question ■	■ Good afternoon, everyone. When I was younger, I didn't enjoy reading. But one day, I found a book that changed my life. My name is Eun-jin, and today, I want to share with you the power of reading.
Using an Interesting Fact ■	■ Good morning, everyone. Have you ever wondered why recycling is so important? My name is Chris, and today, I want to talk to you about how recycling can help protect our planet.
Sharing a Personal Anecdote ■	■ Good morning, everyone. Winston Churchill once said, 'Success is not final, failure is not fatal: It is the courage to continue that counts.' My name is Martin, and I am here to talk about overcoming challenges.
Quoting a Famous Person ■	■ Good morning, everyone. Did you know that eating a healthy diet can increase your life expectancy by up to 10 years? My name is Ji-sun, and today, I want to discuss the benefits of eating healthy."
Stating the Purpose Directly ■	■ Good afternoon, everyone. Today, I want to talk to you about how to stay safe online. My name is Hye-ok, and I am here to provide tips and advice on internet safety.

TIP3   BODY

The body is where the main points and supporting details of the speech are presented. It is usually divided into several paragraphs, each focusing on a specific point.

Common Expressions:
e.g., Firstly, let me tell you about [Point 1].
e.g., For example, [Personal Experience or Fact].
e.g., Another important point is [Point 2].
e.g., Did you know that [Scientific Fact or Statistic]?
e.g., Lastly, let's consider [Point 3].

How to introduce the first point

Start your speech by introducing your first main point. This is something you want to talk about in detail. After introducing the point, give an example or a **personal experience** to make it more relatable and clear.

e.g., Firstly, let me tell you about **my favorite hobby, reading books**. For example, **I started reading when I was seven years old, and now I read a new book every week**.

How to introduce the second point with a fact or statistic

Introduce your second main point. This should be another important topic you want to discuss. To make this point stronger, include a **scientific fact or a statistic**. This adds credibility to your speech and makes it more interesting.

e.g., Another important point is **the benefits of regular exercise**. Did you know that **according to the World Health Organization, regular physical activity can reduce the risk of heart disease by up to 30%**?

How to introduce the third point with an example or explanation

Explanation: Introduce your third main point. This should be the last topic you want to discuss. Provide an **example or a detailed explanation** to support this point. This helps your audience understand why this point is important.

e.g., Lastly, let's consider **the importance of learning new languages. For instance, learning a new language can improve your memory and problem-solving skills, making you smarter and more adaptable in different situations.**

Type of transitions	Examples
Sequential Transitions	First, Next, Finally, Another important point is, Lastly,
Cause and Effect Transitions	Because, As a result, Therefore
Adding Information Transitions	In addition, Also, Moreover, For example, According to

EXERCISE 3. Read the sentences below and fill in the gaps with the appropriate transition words from the list provided. Follow the example

Transition Words
First, Next, Finally Because, As a result, Therefore In addition, Also, Moreover According to

e.g., __First__, let me tell you about why recycling is important.

1. Exercise helps you stay fit. _____, it can reduce stress.

2. Recycling is essential _____ it helps save natural resources.

3. _____ the World Health Organization, regular physical activity can reduce the risk of heart disease by up to 30%.

4. _____, everyone should try to recycle as much as possible.

5. _____, we will discuss how recycling can save energy.

6. Reading books is a great way to learn new things. _____, it can improve your concentration and focus.

7. _____ of recycling, we can reduce the amount of waste in landfills.

8. Eating healthy foods is good for your body. _____, it can improve your mood and energy levels.

CONCLUSION

The conclusion summarizes the main points of the speech and reinforces the message.

Common Expressions:
e.g., In conclusion, I want to emphasize that [Main Message].
e.g., To sum up, [Summary of Key Points].
e.g., Let's remember that [Final Thought].
e.g., I hope you can see why [Topic] is so important.

EXERCISE 4. Read the sentences below. Match them with the appropriate conclusion expression from the list provided. Follow the example.

_____, recycling saves resources, reduces pollution, and conserves energy.

In conclusion, I want to emphasize that

_____ we all have a role to play in protecting our environment.

_____ eating healthy foods can improve our overall well-being.

_____, healthy eating habits lead to a better quality of life.

To sum up,

_____ making small changes to our diet can have big impacts on our health.

_____, exercising regularly helps keep our bodies and minds strong.

CLOSING

The closing thanks the audience and ends the speech on a positive note.

Common Expressions:
e.g., Thank you for listening.
e.g., I appreciate your time and attention.
e.g., Let's all work together to [Call to Action].
e.g., Have a great day!

EXERCISE 5. read the sentences below. Match them with the appropriate closing expression from the list provided. Follow the example.

_____ reduce, reuse, and recycle to protect our environment. ▪   ▪ **Thank you for listening.**
I appreciate your time and attention.

_____. Exercise regularly to keep your body and mind healthy. ▪ **Have a great day.**
I appreciate your time and attention.

_____ save water and help our planet. ▪

_____. Remember, eating healthy is a choice we can make every day. ▪   ▪ **Let's all work together to**

_____ be mindful of our internet safety practices. ▪

_____. Recycling is something we can all do to help our planet. ▪

▪ visual aids can help make their speech more interesting and easier to understand.

▪**Types**

Pictures: Photos or drawings related to the speech topic.

Simple Charts: Bar charts or pie charts that show simple data or steps.

Posters: Posters with key points, illustrations, or diagrams.

▪ **Guidelines for Effective Visual Aids**:

Clarity: Visual aids should be easy to read and understand. For instance, if using text, the font size should be large enough to be seen from the back of the room.

Relevance: They should directly relate to the speech content. For example, if talking about different types of fruit, use pictures of the fruits mentioned.

Simplicity: Use simple images or charts. Too much information can be overwhelming.

▪ **Choosing Visual Aids**:

Pictures: Encourage them to find clear, relevant images related to their topic. For example, if the topic is "My Favorite Hobby," they can use pictures showing them engaging in that hobby.

Charts: Simple charts can be used to show data or steps. For example, if explaining the steps of planting a seed, a chart can show each step in order.

Posters: Teach them to create posters with key points or illustrations. For example, a poster for a speech about healthy eating could show the food pyramid.

▪ **Designing Visual Aids**:

Text: Use large, clear fonts. Keep text minimal. For example, instead of writing "The rainforest is home to many animals such as monkeys, birds, snakes, and insects," a simple bullet point list like "Rainforest Animals: Monkeys, Birds, Snakes, Insects" would be more effective.

Colors: Use contrasting colors to make the text and images stand out. For example, using a dark background with light text can make the text more readable.

Layout: Arrange elements neatly. Teach them to balance text and images on the visual aid. For example, placing an image on one side and the corresponding text on the other side can make it easier to follow.

DEEP DIVE

A. Read the letter below. Compare it with the Model Text. Discuss with your partner about the given text.

Keeping Our Water Clean: Our Duty and Future**

Today, I want to talk to you about something very important: keeping our water clean.

Keeping our water clean is not just about big actions. Small actions, like not littering and using less plastic, make a big difference. We need to think about how our actions affect the water and work together to protect it.

I want to encourage all of you to take the opportunity to protect our water. It is our duty to ensure that future generations can enjoy clean and healthy water. Let's work together to make every effort meaningful and support our environment.

Thank you for listening, and let's all do our part to keep our water clean!

B. Read the Model Text. Underline **Tip1–5** in the text.

SPEECH SCRIPT WRITING STRUCTURE

Process of Writing a Blog Post: (1) **Start with a Title**. The title captures the essence of the speech and the main theme. (2) **Begin with an Introduction** to sets the stage, introduces the speaker, and provides context for the story. Greet your audience, introduce yourself, and give a brief overview of what your speech will be about.

(3) **In the body paragraph,** introduce a personal experience and highlight the importance of your topic. Scientific facts can be discussed in the paragraph. Provide figures and theory. You can add more examples and explanations here. (4) **The conclusion** reinforces the main message and leaves the audience with a powerful takeaway. Restate the main lesson, summarize your key points, and end with an inspirational message.

(5) **Thank** your audience for their attention and give a final, warm farewell. **End with a Call to Action.** Use a positive note.

Title   {

Introduction   *Good [morning/afternoon/evening], everyone*. Today, I want to talk to you about something very important: [Topic]. My name is [Your Name], and I am here to discuss how [Topic] can improve our lives.

Body   **Firstly,** let me tell you about [Point 1]. For example, [Personal Experience or Fact].

Another important point is [Point 2]. Did you know that [Scientific Fact or Statistic]?

Lastly, let's consider [Point 3]. [Example or Explanation].

Conclusion   ***In conclusion,*** I want to emphasize that [Main Message]. To sum up, [Summary of Key Points]. Let's remember that [Final Thought].

Closing   ***Thank you for listening.*** I appreciate your time and attention. Let's all work together to [Call to Action]. Have a great day!

A Few Days Later

Comic made at Pixton.com

Reading about different cultures in class was **_an eye-opening experience_**.

Seeing the stars through a telescope was **_an eye-opening experience_**.

People use an **_eye-opening experience_** to describe something that teaches us a lot and helps us see things in a new way. When you learn something new that surprises you, understand something better after an event, or have an experience that changes your perspective, it is considered an **_eye-opening experience._**

Before an **_eye-opening experience_**, use the "ing" form of a verb and be verb to describe the activity that caused the experience.

e.g., Traveling to a new country was an **_eye-opening experience._**

e.g., Trying traditional food from another country was an **_eye-opening experience_**

EXERCISE 7. Read the given situations. Write your own sentences with **_an eye-opening experience._** Follow the example.

Situation	
e.g., Visiting a new place	e.g., Visiting the zoo for the first time was an eye-opening experience for me.
1. Learning in class	→
2. Helping at home	→

EXERCISE 8. Read the situations and write your own sentences with **an eye-opening experience.** Follow the example.

e.g., You learned about how people lived in the past when you were talking to your grandparents. What will you say?

→ Talking to my grandparents about their childhood was an eye-opening experience.

1. You discovered how fun and interesting science experiments can be in a science fair.
What will you say?

→_____

2. You experienced new foods, music, and traditions from different cultures in a cultural festival.
What will you say?

→_____

3. You want to show your excitement about being involved in the science fair.
What will you say?

→_____

EXERCISE 9. Write your own sentences using **an eye-opening experience.**

1._____

2._____

3._____

4._____

DEEP DIVE

A. Read the Model Text again. Why did the writer say **an eye-opening experience**? Discuss with your partner.

An m dash (–) is a long dash used in writing to add extra information or emphasize a point. It's longer than a hyphen (-) and often used in pairs or alone.

Comic made at Pixton.com

Why Use an M Dash (—)?

People use an M Dash (—) to add extra information or emphasize important parts of a sentence. It helps make the sentence clearer and more interesting.

1. Adding Extra Information: Use an m dash to include extra details or explanations in your sentence.
e.g., We went to the park—it was a sunny day—to play soccer.
e.g., She brought her pet hamster—it's so cute—to school.

2. Creating Emphasis: Use an m dash to highlight important information.
e.g., The winner of the race—everyone was surprised—was the new student.
e.g., The concert was amazing—the best I've ever seen.

How to Use an m dash?

1. Use **two m dashes (one on each side) to set off extra information in the middle** of a sentence.

2. Use **one m dash at the end of a sentence to add a surprising or important detail.**

e.g., We went on a field trip ~~to the museum.~~ [The museum was really interesting].

→We went on a field trip—the museum was really interesting.

e.g., My dad cooked dinner last night. ~~My dad~~ [works as a chef].

→My dad—who works as a chef—cooked dinner last night.

e.g., My teacher told us an interesting story. ~~She is~~ [Mrs. Smith].

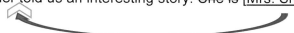

→My teacher—Mrs. Smith—told us an interesting story.

EXERCISE 11. Read the sentence. Add an m dash (—) in each sentence. Follow the examples.

Adding Extra Information	
Without an m dash (—)	**With an m dash (—)**
e.g., Our teacher is Mrs. Brown. He is very kind	e.g., Our teacher—Mrs. Brown—is very kind
e.g., The book was filled with exciting adventures. It kept me reading all night.	
e.g., We visited the museum. It is the one with the dinosaur exhibit.	
Creating Emphasis	
Without an m dash (—)	**With an m dash (—)**
e.g., She sang beautifully. She was like a professional singer.	e.g., She sang beautifully—like a professional singer.
e.g., He finished his homework in just one night. It was the whole project.	
e.g., The cat chased the mouse. It was the one with the white fur.	

EXERCISE 12. Read the Model text. Find an m dash (—) and underline. Think why the writer uses an m dash (—). Work with your partner.

DEEP DIVE

A. When we see an m dash (—) in the sentence, is it possible to guess the function of it at a glance? Discuss with your partner.

MORE EXERCISE FOR GRAMMAR1

Exercise 1. Read the sentence. Add an m dash (—) in each sentence.

I love playing soccer. It is my favorite sport.

→_____

My brother is only eight years old. He can solve a Rubik's Cube.

→_____

We visited the zoo last weekend. The elephants were my favorite.

→_____

My mom makes the best cookies. They are always so delicious.

→_____

I have a pet dog. His name is Max.

→_____

The movie was exciting. I couldn't take my eyes off the screen.

→_____

My best friend Emily. She lives next door.

→_____

I got a new bike for my birthday. It's red and shiny.

→_____

The concert was held in the park. It was amazing.

→_____

11

Comic made at Pixton.com

Present Perfect Tense

1. Form: [have/has] + [past participle]

2. Usage: To express actions that happened at an unspecified time in the past or that started in the past and continue to the present.

3. Examples:

e.g., I **have finished** my homework.
e.g., She **has visited** Paris.
e.g., They **have lived** here for five years.

Three Main Uses of the Present Perfect Tense:

1. For Actions That Happened at an Unspecified Time in the Past:

Use the present perfect tense when the specific time of the action is not important or not mentioned.

e.g., I **have visited** Paris.
e.g., She **has read** that book.
e.g., They **have seen** this movie.

2. For Actions That Started in the Past and Continue to the Present:

Use the present perfect tense for actions that began in the past and are still happening now.

e.g., I **have lived** here for five years.
e.g., She **has worked** at the school since last year.
e.g., I **have played** soccer since I was six.

3. For Actions That Have a Result in the Present:

Use the present perfect tense to show that a past action has a present consequence or result.

e.g., I **have lost** my keys (and now I can't find them).
e.g., She **has finished** her homework (so she is free now).
e.g., They **have cleaned** the house (and now it looks great).

Comic made at Pixton.com

1. The Function of "have/has" in the Perfect Tense

： In the present perfect tense, 'have' serves to form the tense and does not have any meaning by itself.

2. The Function of Past Participles in the Perfect Tense

Completing the Verb Phrase:

The past participle combines with the auxiliary verb "have" to form a complete verb phrase that indicates the perfect aspect. This combination shows that an action was completed before the current moment (present perfect) or before another action in the past (past perfect).

Expressing Completed Actions:

The past participle indicates that the action of the verb is completed. When paired with "have," it provides information about when the action was completed relative to other events or times.

3. Difference Between Past Simple Tense and Present Perfect Tense

Past Simple Tense:

- Used to talk about actions that happened at a specific time in the past.
- The action is completed and there is no connection to the present.

Present Perfect Tense:

- Used to talk about actions that happened at an unspecified time in the past or started in the past and continue to the present.
- The action has a connection to the present or its result is relevant now.

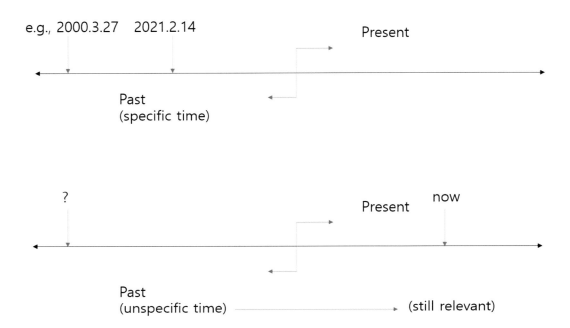

Comparison of Examples:

Past Simple
e.g., I visited Paris last year.
This sentence talks about a specific time in the past. You visited Paris last year. The action is complete, and we know when it happened. "Last year" tells us exactly when you visited Paris. It happened in the past, and it is finished.

Present Perfect
e.g., I have visited Paris.
This sentence talks about an experience at an unspecified time in the past. The action of visiting Paris is still relevant now. We don't know exactly when you visited Paris, but we know that at some point, you have been there. It is an experience you have had.

EXERCISE 17. Go to p.47 and check three functions of the present perfect tense. Complete the sentences using the present perfect tense and figure out what it is used for. Follow the example.

e.g., I ___ (visit) the new museum.	→I have visited the new museum. **(For Actions That Happened at an Unspecified Time in the Past)**
1. She ___ (finish) her project.	→ ( )
2. They ___ (live) in this city for ten years.	→ ( )
3. He ___ (lose) his wallet.	→ ( )
4. We ___ (know) each other since first grade.	→ ( )
5. I ___ (eat) dinner already.	→ ( )

EXERCISE 18. Read the given sentences. Find out and circle if the tense is past simple tense or present perfect tense.

e.g., She (has visited / visited) the museum three times.

1.. They (watched / have watched) a movie on Saturday.

2. I (have eaten / ate) sushi before.

3. She (played / has played) the piano at the concert last week.

4. They (have learned / learned) about space in their last class.

5. I (have read / read) that book.

MORE EXERCISE FOR GRAMMAR2-1

EXERCISE 1. Complete the sentences using the present perfect tense and figure out what it is used for. Follow the example.

1. She ___ (work) here for three months.	→ ( )
2. They ___ (find) their cat.	→ ( )
3. He ___ (write) three books.	→ ( )
4. We ___ (clean) the classroom.	→ ( )
5. They ___ (be) to the new museum several times.	→ ( )

EXERCISE 2. Read the given sentences. Find out and circle if the tense is past simple tense or present perfect tense.

1. She (worked / has worked) here for three months.

2. They (lived / have lived) in this city for five years.

3. I (finished / have finished) my homework already.

4. He (visited / has visited) many countries in his lifetime.

5. We (knew / have known) each other since kindergarten.

MORE EXERCISE FOR GRAMMAR2-2

EXERCISE 1. Look at the picture. Complete sentences using past simple tense or present perfect tense.

swim – swam - swum

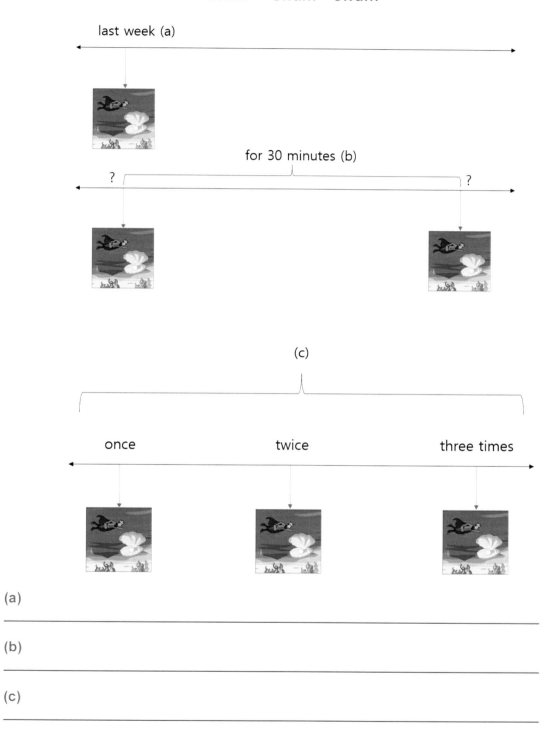

(a)

_____

(b)

_____

(c)

_____

DEEP DIVE

A. When do people use *present perfect tense* in sentences? Discuss with your partner.

B. What *present perfect tense* is used in the Model text? What is the advantage of using *present perfect tense* in the sentences? Discuss with your partner.

HANDS-ON ACTIVITIES

A. Look at the picture. Write sentences using given words. Follow the example.

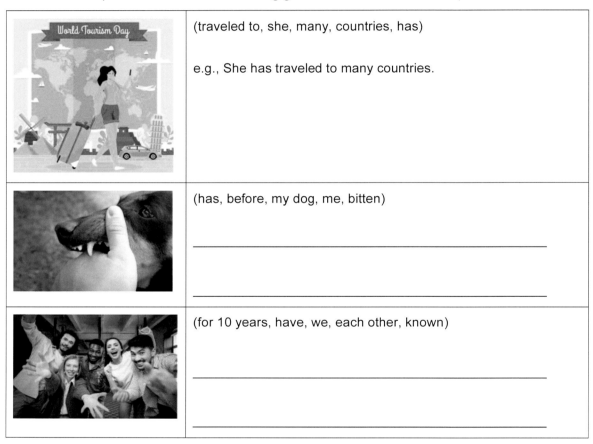

World Tourism Day	(traveled to, she, many, countries, has) e.g., She has traveled to many countries.
	(has, before, my dog, me, bitten) _____ _____
	(for 10 years, have, we, each other, known) _____ _____

B. Write your own sentences with *the present perfect tense.* Work with your partner.

1._____

2._____

3._____

[CLASS7] WRITE WITH YOUR TEACHER 1	The purpose of this task is for you to practice a speech script.

You are writing a speech script to tell the importance of recycling.

Write a speech script that should include:

• title,

• who you are,

• what is the purpose of the speech

• your experiences, scientific facts or statistics, and examples with proper transitions,

• conclusion and closing

• use *an eye-opening experience* appropriately.

• use *the present perfect tense* appropriately.

GAPS

Genre:		Purpose:	
Audience:		Style:	

WRITE

_____	Title: _____
_____	Good afternoon, everyone. Today_____ _____: recycling. My name is _____ _____, and I am here to discuss how recycling can help protect our environment.
_____	_____, let me tell you about why recycling is essential._____, did you know that recycling one ton of paper can save 17 trees? This simple action can make a big difference.
	_____ recycling reduces pollution. According to scientists, recycling plastic saves up to 88% of the energy required to produce plastic from raw materials.
	_____, let's consider how recycling can save money. Many communities earn money by selling recycled materials, which can be used to fund local projects.
_____	_____, recycling is crucial for protecting our environment, reducing pollution, and saving money. Let's remember that small actions like recycling can have a big impact.
_____	_____. _____ Let's all work together to make recycling a part of our daily lives. Have a great day!

CHECKLIST

- Did I write a title? _____
- Did I mention who I am? _____
- Did I mention what is my purpose of the speech? _____
- Did I add your experiences, scientific facts or statistics, and examples with proper transitions? _____
- Does the script have a conclusion and closing? _____
- Did I use *an eye-opening experience* appropriately? _____
- Did I use *the present perfect tense* appropriately? _____

WRITE WITH YOUR TEACHER 2	The purpose of this task is for you to practice blog posting.

You are writing a speech script to tell the importance of your topic.

Write a speech script that should include:

• title,

• who you are,

• what is your purpose of the speech

• your experiences, scientific fact or statistics and examples with proper transitions,

• conclusion and closing

• use **an eye-opening experience** appropriately.

• use **the present perfect tense** appropriately.

GAPS

Genre:		Audience:	
Purpose:		Style:	

PREWRITING

DRAFT

FINAL DRAFT

CHECKLIST

- Did I write a title? _____
- Did I mention who I am? _____
- Did I mention what is my purpose of the speech? _____
- Did I add your experiences, scientific facts or statistics, and examples with proper transitions? _____
- Does the script have a conclusion and closing? _____
- Did I use *an eye-opening experience* appropriately? _____
- Did I use *the present perfect tense* appropriately? _____

Formative Assessment: HOMEWORK

HOMEWORK DAY 1	KEYWORDS

1. Fill in the blanks with the words in the box below. You might need to change the form of the words (*e.g., play > playing, plays, or played*). The words might be used more than once or they might not be used at all.

> unforgettable, relationship, memorable, sightseeing, support, throughout, meaningful, fulfill, connect, intimidating

Title: Keeping Our Water Clean: Our Duty and Future

Good afternoon, everyone. Today, I want to talk to you about something very important: keeping our water clean. My name is Dong-hyun. I had the _____ opportunity to learn about the importance of clean water.

Last year, my family and I went to a beautiful lake for a picnic. The water was clear, and we could see fish swimming. We had fun swimming and playing by the shore. But when we returned there this summer, the lake was dirty, and there was trash everywhere. It was a sad and eye-opening experience for me.

_____ my life, I have learned that clean water is essential for our health and the environment. I realized that we all have a _____ with water—it _____ us, and we need to _____ it too. According to the World Health Organization, 1 in 3 people worldwide do not have access to safe drinking water.

My school takes us on a _____ trip to a local river every year. We saw how pollution from factories and trash affected the water and wildlife. It was _____ to see how much damage we humans can do. But this trip was also _____ because it showed me how important it is to keep our water clean. At school, I joined an environmental club. We worked on projects to clean up local streams and educate others about the importance of clean water. This gave me a chance to _____ with my classmates and work together for a good cause. It felt _____ to make a positive impact.

Keeping our water clean is not just about big actions. Small actions, like not littering and using less plastic, make a big difference. We need to think about how our actions affect the water and work together to protect it.

In sum up, I want to encourage all of you to take the opportunity to protect our water. It is our duty to ensure that future generations can enjoy clean and healthy water. Let's work together to make every effort _____ and _____ our environment.

Thank you for listening, and let's all do our part to keep our water clean!

1. Fill in the blanks with the words in the box below. You might need to change the form of the words (*e.g., play > playing, plays, or played*). The words might be used more than once or they might not be used at all.

---

unforgettable, relationship, memorable, sightseeing, support, throughout, meaningful, fulfill, connect, intimidating

---

Title: Keeping Our Air Clean: Our Duty for a Healthy Future

Good afternoon, everyone. Today, I want to talk to you about something very important: keeping our air clean. My name is Alice. I had the _____ opportunity to learn about the importance of clean air.

When I was younger, my family and I went on a _____ trip to a big city. The tall buildings and busy streets were exciting, but the air was full of smoke and pollution. It was hard to breathe, and I felt tired quickly. This experience showed me how important clean air is for our health.

Throughout my life, I have learned that clean air is essential for everyone. We have a special _____ with the air we breathe—it _____ us and keeps us alive. But when the air is dirty, it can make us sick and unhappy. Dirty air can cause health problems like asthma and lung disease.

Last year, our school organized a project to plant trees around our neighborhood. Trees help clean the air by taking in carbon dioxide and giving out oxygen. One large tree can provide a day's supply of oxygen for up to four people. Working with my classmates to plant trees was fun and _____. We all felt _____ to each other and to nature. It was a _____l way to make our air cleaner and healthier.

Sometimes, keeping the air clean can seem _____. But even small actions can make a big difference. For example, we can ride bikes instead of driving cars, or we can save energy by turning off lights when we don't need them. These simple steps help reduce pollution and keep our air clean.

In summary, I want to encourage all of you to take the opportunity to protect our air. Remember, it is our duty to ensure that future generations can enjoy clean and healthy air. Let's work together to make every effort _____ and _____ our environment.

Thank you for listening, and let's all do our part to keep our air clean!

2. Read again and find the GAPS of the given text above. Then complete the table below.

Genre:	Audience:
Purpose:	Style:

3. Write about the structure of the speech script.

4. Write about the SEVOC.

1. Fill in the blanks with the words in the box below. You might need to change the form of the words (*e.g., play > playing, plays, or played*). The words might be used more than once or they might not be used at all.

> unforgettable, relationship, memorable, sightseeing, support, throughout, meaningful, fulfill, connect, intimidating

Title: Let's Work Hard to Recycle: Our Duty for a Better Future

Good afternoon, everyone. Today, I want to talk to you about something very important: recycling. My name is So-yen. Let me tell you a story about an eye-opening experience that made me realize how crucial recycling is for our planet.

When I was younger, my family and I went on a _____ hike in the mountains. The views were beautiful, and the air was fresh. But as we walked, we saw trash along the trail. It was sad to see such a beautiful place spoiled by litter. This experience showed me how important it is to recycle and take care of our environment.

_____ my life, I have learned that recycling is essential for protecting our planet. We have a special _____ with nature—it _____ us, and we need to _____ it too. Recycling helps keep our environment clean and healthy.

At school, I joined an environmental club. We worked on projects to promote recycling and educate others about its importance. Working with my classmates to collect recyclables and reduce waste was fun and _____. We all felt _____ to each other and to our mission. It was a _____ way to make a positive impact. Recycling just one ton of paper can save 17 trees and 7,000 gallons of water.

Sometimes, recycling can seem _____. But even small actions can make a big difference. For example, we can sort our trash at home, use reusable bags, and encourage our friends and family to recycle. These simple steps help reduce waste and keep our environment clean.

Finally, I want to encourage all of you to take the opportunity to recycle. Remember, it is our duty to ensure that future generations can enjoy a clean and healthy environment. Let's work together to make every effort _____ I and _____ our planet.

Thank you for listening, and let's all do our part to recycle and keep our world beautiful!

2. Write about 5 and additional tips for writing a speech script.

1. Fill in the blanks with the words in the box below. You might need to change the form of the words (*e.g., play > playing, plays, or played*). The words might be used more than once or they might not be used at all.

> unforgettable, relationship, memorable, sightseeing, support, throughout, meaningful, fulfill, connect, intimidating

Title: Let's Reduce Eating Junk Food and Have a Healthy Diet

Good afternoon, everyone. Did you know that eating too much junk food can lead to obesity and other health problems? My name is Rosa. Let me share a story about an eye-opening experience I had that changed the way I think about food.

When I was younger, I loved eating hamburgers and fries. One day, I ate too many hamburgers at a party. Later, I felt very sick and had a bad stomachache. This experience showed me how harmful junk food can be to our health.

_____ my life, I have learned that what we eat affects how we feel. We have a special _____ with food—it _____ us and gives us energy. But junk food can make us feel tired and unhealthy. Eating healthy food helps us stay strong and happy. According to the World Health Organization, eating at least five servings of fruits and vegetables each day can reduce the risk of serious health issues.

Last year, our school organized a trip to a farm. It was a _____ tour where we saw how fruits and vegetables are grown. We learned that fresh, natural food is much better for us than junk food. This trip was very _____ because it showed me the importance of choosing healthy food.

Sometimes, it can be _____ to change our eating habits. But small steps can make a big difference. For example, we can eat more fruits and vegetables and drink more water. These simple changes can help us feel better and stay healthy.

Finally, I want to encourage all of you to take the opportunity to eat healthier. Remember, it is our responsibility to take care of our bodies. Let's _____ each other in making healthy choices and _____ with good food that _____ our needs.

Thank you for listening, and let's all do our part to reduce eating junk food and have a healthy diet!

2. When can we use *an eye-opening experience*? Give one example that the expression can be used.

3. Read the situation and use an *eye-opening experience* in complete sentences.

Situation 1: You try cooking a healthy meal with your family and discover new delicious recipes.

_____.

Situation 2: You meet someone from a different country and learn about their culture and traditions

_____.

Situation 3: You watch a documentary about space and realize how vast and incredible the universe is.

_____.

Situation 4: You participate in a beach cleanup and see the amount of trash that washes up on shore.

_____.

Situation 5: You visit a recycling center and see how much waste can be turned into new products.

_____.

1. Fill in the blanks with the words in the box below. You might need to change the form of the words (*e.g., play > playing, plays, or played*). The words might be used more than once or they might not be used at all.

> unforgettable, relationship, memorable, sightseeing, support, throughout, meaningful, fulfill, connect, intimidating, eye-opening experience, —

Title: Let's Reduce Using Cell phones in Bed: A Healthy Choice**

Good afternoon, everyone. Today, I want to talk to you about something very important: reducing the use of cell phones in bed. My name is Na-rin. Let me start by asking you a question: Have you ever felt really tired and unfocused at school because you stayed up too late on your phone? I have, and I want to share why it's important to use our cell phones less before bed.

When I was younger, I loved using my cell phone in bed. I would play games, watch videos, and chat with friends. One night, I stayed up very late using my phone. The next day, I felt tired, couldn't focus in class, and even had a headache. This experience showed me how harmful it can be to use cell phones in bed.

_____ my life, I have learned that good sleep is essential for our health. We have a special _____ with sleep_____it _____ us, helps us grow, and keeps us healthy. However, using cell phones in bed can disrupt our sleep and make us feel tired and unhappy.

Last year, our school took us on a _____ trip to a science museum. We learned about how the blue light from cell phones can trick our brains into thinking it's daytime, making it harder for us to fall asleep. According to sleep experts, blue light from screens can reduce melatonin production, a hormone that helps us sleep. This scientific fact made me realize how important it is to reduce cellphone use before bed. It was a _____ lesson that connected directly to my own experiences.

Sometimes, it can be _____ to change our habits. But even small steps can make a big difference. For example, we can put our phones away an hour before bed and read a book or listen to calming music instead. These simple changes can help us get better sleep and feel more energetic throughout the day.

Finally, I want to encourage all of you to take the opportunity to reduce using cell phones in bed. Remember, it is our responsibility to take care of our health. Let's _____ each other in making healthy choices and _____ with better habits that _____ our needs for good sleep.

Thank you for listening, and let's all do our part to reduce using cell phones in bed and have a healthier lifestyle!

2. Write about the function of _an M dash (—)_.

3. Read the sentences. Change the sentences using an _M dash (—)_. Follow the examples.

e.g., My sister plays the piano beautifully. She is a talented musician.
→ My sister—a talented musician—plays the piano beautifully

1. There's only one person I trust. I only trust my best friend.
→

2. She made the cake. Everyone loved the delicious cake.
→

3. The movie was exciting. I couldn't take my eyes off the screen.
→

4. My dog loves to meet new people. He is very friendly.
→

5. I love playing soccer. It is my favorite sport.
→

1. Fill in the blanks with the words in the box below. You might need to change the form of the words (*e.g., play > playing, plays, or played*). The words might be used more than once or they might not be used at all.

unforgettable, relationship, memorable, sightseeing, support, throughout, meaningful, fulfill, connect, intimidating, eye-opening experience, —

Title: Embracing Our Differences: Why Respecting Each Other Matters

Good afternoon, everyone. Imagine a world where everyone looked, thought, and acted the same. It would be so boring and dull, right? Today, I want to talk to you about something very important: understanding and respecting our differences. My name is Hyo-seon. I learned something truly amazing about why we should value and respect each other's unique qualities.

When I was younger, I had a friend named Alex. We were very close, but one day, we had a big fight because we didn't agree on something. It was a very sad and lonely time for me. I missed my friend and felt very bad. This experience taught me how important it is to respect each other's opinions and differences.

_____ my life, I have learned that everyone is unique. We all have different thoughts, feelings, and ways of seeing the world. According to research, having diverse friendships helps us develop better problem-solving skills and can even improve our overall happiness. Respecting each other's differences helps us _____ and _____ each other, making our _____ more _____.

Last year, our school took us on a _____ trip to a cultural festival. We saw different performances, tasted various foods, and learned about many cultures. It was an _____ that showed me how beautiful and enriching our differences can be. This trip was very meaningful because it made me realize that understanding and respecting each other makes our world a better place.

Sometimes, it can be _____ to accept differences, especially when we don't understand them. But we should always try to listen and learn from each other. This helps us build strong and _____ _____. For example, after my fight with Alex, we talked about our feelings and tried to understand each other. We made up and became even closer friends.

Finally, I want to encourage all of you to take the opportunity to respect and appreciate our differences. Remember, it is our responsibility to _____ each other and make our _____ stronger. Let's work together to make every connection _____ and full of respect.

Thank you for listening, and let's all do our part to understand and respect everyone's differences!

2. Write about how *Present Perfect Tense* works in the sentences.

3. Read the text. Underline time *Present Perfect Tense* and circle reason *Present Perfect Tense*.

Good afternoon, everyone. Today, I want to talk to you about something very important: keeping safety rules when you go swimming. My name is Hye-rin and I had an unforgettable experience that taught me why safety rules are so important.

Last summer, my family and I went on a sightseeing trip to the beach. The weather was perfect, and the water looked so inviting. My friends and I were very excited to swim. However, we didn't pay attention to the safety rules. One of my friends swam too far out and got caught in a strong current. It was a very intimidating and scary moment for all of us. Thankfully, the lifeguard was there to help and brought my friend back safely. This eye-opening experience showed me how important it is to follow safety rules when swimming.

Throughout my life, I have learned that safety rules are there to protect us. They help us enjoy our time in the water without getting hurt. We have a special relationship with water—it can be fun and relaxing, but it can also be dangerous if we are not careful. Following safety rules makes our swimming experience both safe and memorable.

I have also joined a swimming club at school. Our coach has always emphasized the importance of safety. We learned to swim with a buddy, to stay in designated areas, and to always listen to the lifeguard. These rules are simple but very meaningful. They support us and help us fulfill our goal of staying safe while having fun. Our coach's lessons have helped me connect better with my friends and support each other while swimming.

Sometimes, safety rules can seem intimidating or annoying. But they are there for a reason—to keep us safe. By following them, we can avoid accidents and have a great time. For example, always check the water depth before diving, and never swim alone. These small steps make a big difference.

Finally, I want to encourage all of you to remember and follow the safety rules when you go swimming. It is our responsibility to keep ourselves and our friends safe. Let's support each other and make our swimming experiences unforgettable and safe. Remember, following the rules is a way to show that we care for and respect each other.

Thank you for listening, and let's all do our part to stay safe and enjoy swimming!

1. Fill in the blanks with the words in the box below. You might need to change the form of the words (*e.g., play > playing, plays, or played*). The words might be used more than once or they might not be used at all.

> unforgettable, relationship, memorable, sightseeing, support, throughout, meaningful, fulfill, connect, intimidating, eye-opening experience, —

Title: Let's Not Waste Electricity: A Smart Choice**

Good afternoon, everyone. Imagine if you woke up one day and there was no electricity_____no lights, no internet, and no way to play your favorite video games. Sounds pretty tough, right? Today, I want to talk to you about something very important: not wasting electricity. My name is Seo-young. Let me tell you about an _____ experience that taught me the importance of saving electricity.

When I was younger, I loved playing video games. I would leave my game console and TV on all day, even when I wasn't playing. One day, there was a power outage in our neighborhood because too many people were using too much electricity. We had no lights, no internet, and no way to cook dinner. It was a very uncomfortable and _____ for me. This showed me how harmful it can be to waste electricity.

Throughout my life, I have learned that electricity is essential for our daily activities. We have a special relationship with electricity_____it _____ us by powering our homes and gadgets. But when we waste electricity, it can harm the environment and cause problems like power outages.

Last year, our school took us on a _____ trip to a science museum. We learned about how generating electricity can cause pollution. The more electricity we use, the more pollution we create. This scientific fact made me realize how important it is to save electricity. It was a _____ lesson that _____ directly to my own experiences.

Sometimes, it can be _____ to change our habits. But even small steps can make a big difference. For example, we can turn off the lights when we leave a room, unplug chargers when we're not using them, and use energy-saving bulbs. Studies show that using energy-saving bulbs can reduce energy use by 75% compared to traditional bulbs. These simple changes can help us save electricity and protect our environment.

Finally, I want to encourage all of you to take the opportunity to save electricity. Remember, it is our responsibility to take care of our planet and our future. Let's _____ each other in making smart choices and _____ with better habits that _____ our needs without wasting resources.

Thank you for listening, and let's all do our part to not waste electricity and keep our world bright and clean!

HOMEWORK DAY 7	PRACTICE FOR YOUR INDEPENDENT WRITING

You are writing a speech script to tell the importance of your topic.

Write a speech script that should include:

• title,

• who you are,

• what is the purpose of the speech

• your experiences, scientific facts or statistics, and examples with proper transitions,

• conclusion and closing

• use *an eye-opening experience* appropriately.

• use *the present perfect tense* appropriately.

GAPS

Genre		Audience	
Purpose		Style	

PREWRITING

DRAFT

Final Draft

Checklist for Revising and Editing

• Did I write a title? _____

• Did I mention who I am? _____

• Did I mention what is my purpose of the speech? _____

• Did I add your experiences, scientific facts or statistics, and examples with proper transitions? _____

• Does the script have a conclusion and closing? _____

• Did I use *an eye-opening experience* appropriately? _____

• Did I use *the present perfect tense* appropriately? _____

Summative Assessment: Writing Portfolio Assignment (WPA)

INDEPENDENT WRITING	The purpose of this task is for you to practice writing a speech script.

You are writing a speech script to tell the importance of your topic.

Write a speech script that should include:

• title,

• who you are,

• what is the purpose of the speech

• your experiences, scientific facts or statistics, and examples with proper transitions,

• conclusion and closing

• use *an eye-opening experience* appropriately.

• use *the present perfect tense* appropriately.

GAPS

Genre:		Audience:	
Purpose:		Style:	

PREWRITING

DRAFT

FINAL DRAFT

CHECKLIST FOR REVISING AND EDITING

- Did I write a title? _____
- Did I mention who I am? _____
- Did I mention what is my purpose of the speech? _____
- Did I add your experiences, scientific facts or statistics, and examples with proper transitions? _____
- Does the script have a conclusion and closing? _____
- Did I use *an eye-opening experience* appropriately? _____
- Did I use *the present perfect tense* appropriately? _____

SPEECH SCRIPT RUBRIC FOR MODULE 10

BAND	GENRE FEATURES	COHERENCE AND COHESION	LEXICAL RESOURCE	GRAMMATICAL RANGE AND ACCURACY OF AS, AND A COLON	TASK ACHIEVEMENT
3	Correctly uses the typical structure of a speech script. Includes an appropriate title and details with politeness.	Well-organized, with clear connections between sentences, and uses transitions to help readers better understand.	Utilizes a simple range of vocabulary correctly and effectively, suitable for A1 level.	Uses basic grammatical structures, and punctuation, especially *M dash, Present perfect tense, and an eye-opening experience* accurately and effectively, with no or very few errors.	Fully completes the task by appropriately addressing all aspects of the speech script writing prompt with simple yet accurate supporting ideas.
2	Partially includes speech script genre features with polite sentences, but some key elements may be missing or inadequately executed.	Generally well-organized but may lack some coherence in sentence connections with transitions.	Uses some suitable vocabulary but may lack variety or contain some words not used correctly.	Uses grammatical structures, and punctuation, especially *M dash, Present perfect tense, and an eye-opening* but may contain errors that sometimes obstruct understanding.	Partially completes the task by addressing some aspects of the prompt with a few relevant but simple supporting ideas; however, some aspects might be lacking.
1	Largely misses speech script genre features, and includes inappropriate elements for instruction.	Disorganized or lacks logical flow from one sentence to another.	Shows a lack of vocabulary variety or contains many words used incorrectly.	Lacks accuracy in the use of punctuation, *M dash, Present perfect tense, and an eye-opening* make the text difficult to understand.	Largely fails to address the speech script writing prompt appropriately or lacks the necessary supporting ideas.
0	The speech script is not written				

Formative Evaluation: Teachers' diaries and records

Name of student (grade in school)		
Date	Diary	Record

Summative Evaluation: Student Survey Questionnaire

Rating scale questions		1 = "strongly disagree" 5 = "strongly agree"				
1	The goals of the course were clear and appropriate.	1	2	3	4	5
2	I was clearly stated my responsibilities and course requirements at the beginning.	1	2	3	4	5
3	The assessment used in the course was appropriate and fair.	1	2	3	4	5
4	The materials used in the course were appropriate and useful.	1	2	3	4	5
5	The texts and topics covered were interesting and relevant.	1	2	3	4	5
6	I was given clear instructions and explained things well.	1	2	3	4	5
7	I was given enough chances to write.	1	2	3	4	5
8	The lessons contained an appropriate variety of activities.	1	2	3	4	5
Open-ended questions						
9	What did you like most about the course?					
10	What did you like least about the course?					

Guided by Growth

This section provides a concise introduction to the key concepts and interrelations of TCL, genre writing, and process writing, which form the foundational methodology of this book. A thoughtful and thorough reading of this section is essential, as it will significantly benefit your understanding and participation in the class/

This document is a guide that provides a sample lesson plan to help teachers in their teaching process. Teachers don't have to follow it exactly, and it can be adjusted based on the teacher's experience and the needs of the students.

Using this guide could be very helpful for new teachers or those not very experienced with making lesson plans. It allows teachers to make their own lesson plans suitable for their students and their teaching situation.

This guide supports a detailed and effective way of planning lessons, making teachers more flexible and creative in their teaching strategies. This way, teaching becomes more focused on the students' needs, helping them learn in a way that's best for them.

Often, due to tight class schedules, instructors rush into lessons without clarifying the objectives. This lack of context is a key reason why students might not find the class engaging. By discussing questions and exchanging views with students, educators can leverage their existing knowledge and spark curiosity in the subject matter.

While many Korean English learners might not naturally choose to write diaries in English, I've included a diary module in this book for several reasons. Firstly, it's an excellent way to practice past tenses and improve coherence and cohesion. Many learners find it challenging to freely express their personal experiences and feelings in English, and the diary format can help break down these barriers. Plus, this module offers a chance to explore different ways of expressing time, rather than sticking to just one approach.

Learning keywords is a gradual process, not something that occurs instantly. A learner needs multiple exposures to a word to learn it effectively. The texts within a module generally reuse many of the words, facilitating this repetitive exposure. Additionally, there are more extensive learning resources available in the assignments towards the end of the book, which can be highly beneficial, so be sure to make good use of them. Most vocabulary learning focuses on linking words in Korean and English, but it's also crucial to remember the importance of learners consistently hearing the pronunciation and accent of essential words.

In this book, webtoons play a pivotal role in showcasing why this genre stands out uniquely. Instead of casually browsing through the webtoons, teachers should motivate learners by having them read in groups or participate in role-playing activities. Furthermore, guiding them through the webtoon dialogues will help them understand the essence of the genre and the book's overarching narrative

Ironically, the most common types of English writing that Korean students produce are argumentative and explanatory essays. However, most students have only tried writing argumentative essays without actually learning how to do it properly. SEVOC is a term I created to help remember how to start an argumentative essay, what examples or supporting ideas to include, how to develop the essay without making it boring while increasing its persuasiveness, and how to gradually narrow down to the main argument.

Additionally, in presentations, I have often witnessed situations in the classroom where visual aids are filled with text, leading presenters to read directly from them, which bores the audience. Therefore, I have included some simple tips on how to create effective visual aids.

In this section, I have provided more detailed examples of the concepts briefly explained above. In fact, argumentative writing can be seen as the final destination of writing genres. Therefore, I understand that it might be difficult for students to fully grasp everything I have included. However, I personally believe that there is a significant difference between a student who has encountered these concepts even once and a student who has never seen them at all. Even if they cannot master it now, I hope that knowing and having learned these concepts will provide some help to the students in the future. This is why I have included detailed examples.

I have mentioned before that one of the most important aspects of writing is flow. In argumentative or explanatory essays, the key element that creates flow is transitions. This is something that needs to be taught in Korean as well, especially because the expressions themselves can be difficult and must be used while understanding the context before and after them. Therefore, it requires a lot of practice and cannot be mastered all at once.

Besides the expressions and practice exercises I have provided, I recommend training students with more expressions and exercises.

Here, what we call "Common Sayings" are also widely recognized as "fixed expressions." Learning these as whole patterns, instead of dissecting their grammatical structures, can be more beneficial for learners. When using the expression "깜짝 놀랄," students usually use the word "surprising." To introduce a more vivid expression and to teach the use of hyphens, which they have used when writing names, I included it in the textbook. I thought it might be a fresher alternative to the usual expressions.

Like colons, the em dash is a punctuation mark that students find interesting but rarely have the opportunity to learn about. I included it in the textbook to address this gap. I initially wanted to compare the en dash, em dash, and hyphen, but since they are all straight lines of different lengths and their roles are not simple, I hope to cover this topic more thoroughly in another book if given the chance. I believe that we should not deprive students of learning opportunities, regardless of their skill level. Even a single experience can become a link to further opportunities for that student. The explanatory part is somewhat similar to relative pronouns, so it will be helpful for students who understand relative pronouns. For those who have not yet learned relative pronouns, it will be beneficial when they do.

The present perfect tense, which does not exist in Korean tense expressions, was a major source of confusion for me when I first learned it in school. It was also one of the main reasons I wanted to give up on learning English. Language reflects the culture of its country, much like a big picture. If I had started with the concept that their view of time is different from ours, I might have found it difficult but would not have given up on English. Different does not mean wrong. In our grammar, modal verbs and auxiliary verbs are often taught interchangeably, but I want to emphasize that they are distinctly different types of verbs. The reason I did not mention this here is that I remember the readers of this book are at the A1 level. To put it simply, I explain to my students that the "have" in the present perfect tense is just a container expressing the tense, while the past participle (in foreign contexts, calling it "p.p." is not understood) carries the meaning of the verb. Despite its past form, it has nothing to do with the past. I believe that a deeper explanation of this topic would not only be unnecessary but also harmful to the students.

[닫는 말]

Discover Writing Discover Korea 시리즈는 단순한 영어 학습서가 아닌, 한국 문화의 심장으로의 여행입니다. 이 시리즈 안에서 학습자들과 선생님들은 언어 학습과 문화적 몰입이 동시에 어우러진 독특한 경험을 할 수 있습니다. 일상 생활에서 먼 거리에 있던 그동안의 영어학습과 달리, 이 시리즈는 그 간극을 메워 교육적이면서도 공감 가능한 학습 경험을 제공합니다.

또한, 이 시리즈는 언어 학습에 새로운 시각을 제시합니다. 한국 문화, 관습 및 경험을 영어 교육에 엮음으로써 종합적인 접근 방식으로 언어를 습득할 기회를 제공합니다.

저는 여기에서 멈추지 않고 이 시리즈를 확장하고 한국 문화, 역사 및 현대 생활의 풍부함을 더 깊이 탐구하고 다른 장르로 확장할 계획이며 영어 쓰기교육을 넘어 읽기, 듣기 및 말하기를 포함한 종합적인 자료를 만들고 싶습니다.

흥미진진한 영어와 한국문화의 탐구 여정에 저와 함께 해보시면 어떨까요? 한 페이지 한 페이지마다 다양한 글의 장르와 한국을 탐험하면서 영어쓰기의 즐거움을 다시 발견해보세요. 독자가 되어 주심에 감사드리며, 앞으로의 만남을 기다리겠습니다.

2023 년 10 월 28 일

서은옥 드림

[Epilogue]

The **Discover Writing Discover Korea** series is not just a set of English textbooks; it's a journey into the heart of Korean culture. In these pages, you'll find a unique blend of language learning and cultural immersion. These books bridge the gap that feels distant from our daily lives, making the learning experience not only educational but also relatable.

It offers a fresh perspective on language learning. By weaving Korean culture, customs, and experiences into English education, it provides a holistic approach to language acquisition.

As for the future, my commitment is unwavering. I plan to expand this series, delving deeper into the richness of Korean culture, history, and modern life with other genres. I aim to create a comprehensive resource that not only enhances English writing skills but also reading listening and speaking, delving deeper into the richness of Korean culture, history, and modern life.

So, join me in this exciting journey of language and culture. Rediscover the joy of learning as you explore different genres and Korea, one page at a time. Thank you for your support, and I look forward to sharing more with you in the future.

Sincerely,

Eun-ok Seo

Discover Writing Discover Korea 10

발 행 | 2024년 8월 5일

저 자 | 서은옥

펴낸이 | 한건희

펴낸곳 | 주식회사 부크크

출판사등록 | 2014.07.15(제2014-16호)

주 소 | 서울특별시 금천구 가산디지털1로 119 SK트윈타워 A동 305호

전 화 | 1670-8316

이메일 | info@bookk.co.kr

ISBN | 979-11-410-9962-6

www.bookk.co.kr